# Collins

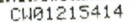

# TREASURE HOUSE

## Pupil Book 2

# Comprehension Skills

Author: Abigail Steel

# HarperCollins Publishers
## 200 — Since 1817

William Collins' dream of knowledge for all began with the publication of his first book in 1819.

A self-educated mill worker, he not only enriched millions of lives, but also founded a flourishing publishing house. Today, staying true to this spirit, Collins books are packed with inspiration, innovation and practical expertise. They place you at the centre of a world of possibility and give you exactly what you need to explore it.

Collins. Freedom to teach.

Published by Collins
An imprint of HarperCollinsPublishers
The News Building
1 London Bridge Street
London
SE1 9GF

HarperCollinsPublishers, 1st Floor, Watermarque Building, Ringsend Road, Dublin 4, Ireland

Browse the complete Collins catalogue at
**www.collins.co.uk**

© HarperCollinsPublishers Limited 2017

10 9 8 7 6

ISBN 978-0-00-823635-9

Publishing Director: Lee Newman
Publishing Manager: Helen Doran
Senior Editor: Hannah Dove
Project Manager: Emily Hooton
Author: Abigail Steel
Development Editor: Hannah Hirst-Dunton
Copy-editor: Tanya Solomons
Proofreader: Tracy Thomas and Gaynor Spry
Cover design and artwork: Amparo Barrera and Ken Vail Graphic Design
Internal design concept: Amparo Barrera
Typesetter: Jouve India Private Ltd
Illustrations: Advocate Art, Beatriz Castro, Aptara and QBS
Production Controller: Rachel Weaver
Printed in Great Britain by Martins the Printers

MIX
Paper from responsible sources
FSC C007454

This book is produced from independently certified FSC paper to ensure responsible forest management.

For more information visit:
www.harpercollins.co.uk/green

## Acknowledgements

The publishers wish to thank the following for permission to reproduce content. Every effort has been made to trace copyright holders and to obtain their permission for the use of copyright materials. The publishers will gladly receive any information enabling them to rectify any error or omission at the first opportunity.

Macmillan for an extract on page 4 from *The Kingfisher Book of Fairy Tales* by Vivian French, text copyright © Vivian French 2004. First published in 2005 by Macmillan Children's Books, an imprint of Pan Macmillan, a division of Macmillan Publishers International Limited; Frances Lincoln Publishers for an extract on page 6 from *Jamil's Clever Cat: A Folk Tale from Bengal* by Fiona French and Dick Newby, Frances Lincoln Ltd, copyright © 2006. Reproduced by permission of Frances Lincoln Ltd; David Higham Associates Ltd for an extract on page 8 from *Tom's Sausage Lion* by Michael Morpurgo, published by Egmont Books Ltd. Reproduced by permission of David Higham Associates Ltd; The Society of Authors for the poem on page 10 'Some One' by Walter de la Mare, published in *The Complete Poems of Walter de la Mare*, 1975. Reproduced by permission of the Literary Trustees of Walter de la Mare and The Society of Authors as their representative; Judith Nicholls for the poem on page 13 'Who's There?' by Judith Nicholls copyright © Judith Nicholls, 2015. Reproduced by kind permission of the author; Usborne Publishing Ltd for an extract on page 17 from *50 Science Things to Make and Do*. Reproduced by permission of Usborne Publishing, 83–85 Saffron Hill, London EC1N 8RT, UK, www.usborne.com, copyright © 2005, 2008 Usborne Publishing Ltd; HarperCollins Publishers Ltd for an extract on page 19 from *The Stone Cutter* by Sean Taylor, copyright © Sean Taylor 2005; and an extract on page 21 from *Your Senses* by Sally Morgan, copyright © Sally Morgan, 2012. Reproduced by permission of HarperCollins Publishers Ltd; and Usborne Publishing Ltd for an extract on page 23 from *Gerbils*. Reproduced by permission of Usborne Publishing, 83–85 Saffron Hill, London EC1N 8RT, UK, www.usborne.com, copyright © 2005, 2008 Usborne Publishing Ltd; HarperCollins Publishers Ltd for an extract on page 25 from *Rumpelstiltskin* by Abie Longstaff, copyright © HarperCollins Publishers Ltd 2015; extract on page 27 from *The Great Chapatti Chase* by Penny Dolan, copyright © Penny Dolan 2015; extract on page 29 from *Mountain Mona* by Vivian French, copyright © Vivian French 2006; extract on page 31 from *If* by Mij Kelly, copyright © Mij Kelly 2012; poem 'Market Day' on page 33 from *Catching Flies* by June Crebbin, copyright © June Crebbin 2012; extract on page 36 from *Landmarks of the World* by Helen Chapman, copyright © Helen Chapman 2015; extract on page 38 from *A Letter to New Zealand* by Alison Hawes, copyright © HarperCollins Publishers Ltd 2005; extract on page 40 from *How to Make Storybooks* by Ros Asquith, copyright © Ros Asquith 2005; extract on page 42 from *How Does It Work?* by Sylvia Karavis and Gill Matthews, copyright © HarperCollins Publishers Ltd 2005; extract on page 44 from *The Cloud Forest* by Nic Bishop, copyright © Nic Bishop 2005; extract on page 46 from *Tiger's Tale* by Michaela Morgan, copyright © Michaela Morgan 2005; extract on page 48 from *The Brave Baby* by Malachy Doyle, copyright © Malachy Doyle 2004; and extract on page 50 from *Bugs* by Sam McBratney, copyright © Sam McBratney 2010. Reproduced by permission of HarperCollins Publishers Ltd.

The publishers would like to thank the following for permission to reproduce photographs:

p.36 (t) Karimhesham/iStock, p.36 (b) Volodymyr Goinyk/Shutterstock, p.37 Fstockfoto/Shutterstock, p.38 MH People/Alamy Stock Photo, p.39 Paul Seheult/Getty Images, all other photos © HarperCollins Publishers Ltd.

# Contents

| | Page |
|---|---|
| Unit 1: Fairy tale: 'Jack and the Beanstalk' | 4 |
| Unit 2: Traditional tale: 'Jamil's Clever Cat' | 6 |
| Unit 3: Contemporary tale: 'Tom's Sausage Lion' | 8 |
| Unit 4: Classic poetry: 'Some One' | 10 |
| Unit 5: Classic poetry: 'Who's There?' | 13 |
| Unit 6: Word play: 'Eletelephony' | 15 |
| Unit 7: Instructions: Be a snake charmer | 17 |
| Review unit 1: Fiction (story): 'The Stone Cutter' | 19 |
| Unit 8: Explanations: 'Seeing the world' | 21 |
| Unit 9: Non-chronological report: Gerbils | 23 |
| Unit 10: Fairy tale: 'Rumpelstiltskin' | 25 |
| Unit 11: Traditional tale: 'The Great Chapatti Chase' | 27 |
| Unit 12: Contemporary tale: 'Mountain Mona' | 29 |
| Unit 13: Classic poetry: 'If' | 31 |
| Unit 14: Contemporary poetry: 'Market Day' | 33 |
| Review unit 2: Non-fiction (information text): 'Landmarks of the World' | 36 |
| Unit 15: Recount: 'A Letter to New Zealand' | 38 |
| Unit 16: Instructions: 'How to Make Storybooks' | 40 |
| Unit 17: Explanation: 'How does a magnetic drawing board work?' | 42 |
| Unit 18: Non-chronological report: 'The Cloud Forest' | 44 |
| Unit 19: Contemporary tale: 'Tiger's Tale' | 46 |
| Unit 20: Traditional tale: 'The Brave Baby' | 48 |
| Review unit 3: Poetry: 'Bugs' | 50 |

**Comprehension** Unit 1

# Fairy tale: 'Jack and the Beanstalk'

**From 'Jack and the Beanstalk' by Vivian French**

Jack's mother took in other people's washing to make a little money, but as she got older she found this harder and harder. Jack was no help to her. He dropped the washing and lost the pegs and forgot to look to see if it was raining. He was much too busy sitting on the doorstep singing '*Dee-dah diddle-di-dee*'.

At last there was no money left at all.

'Jack!' said his mother, and there were tears in her eyes. 'Jack! You must take poor Daisy to market and sell her. Sell her for as much money as you can, for we have nothing left.'

## Get started

Copy the sentences and complete them using words from the story.

1. Jack's mother took in other people's _____ to make a little _____ .

2. As she got older she found this _____ and _____ .

3. At last there was no _____ left at _____ .

4. Jack had to take poor Daisy to _____ and _____ her.

## Try these

Ask a teacher for help with any words in the story you do not know. Write a sentence to answer each question.

1. What was Jack singing?
2. Why did Jack's mother tell him to sell Daisy?
3. Why do you think Jack's mother had tears in her eyes?
4. Who do you think Daisy is?

## Now try these

1. What is Jack like? Write a sentence.
2. Draw a picture of Jack going to the market. Add a sentence to show what Jack is thinking.

**Comprehension** Unit 2

# Traditional tale: 'Jamil's Clever Cat'

**From 'Jamil's Clever Cat' by Fiona French with Nick Newby**

Jamil the weaver lived on the poor side of town. He had a cat called Sardul, a very clever cat. Each night, while Jamil was asleep, Sardul wove material for his master to make into tunics and saris.

One morning, Jamil sighed and said, 'Oh Sardul, if only I could marry the princess who lives in the palace! Then you and I would not have to work our fingers and paws to the bone, and I would be a very happy man.'

Sardul thought for a minute. Then he said, 'Give me the best waistcoat and the most beautiful sari we have made, Master, and I can make your dream come true.'

## Get started

Copy the sentences and complete them using words from the story.

1. Jamil the weaver lived on the _____ side of _____ .
2. He had a _____ called Sardul.
3. Sardul wove _____ for his master to make into _____ and saris.

## Try these

Ask a teacher for help with any words in the story you do not know. Write a sentence to answer each question.

1. What did Sardul do at night?
2. What did Jamil do with the material Sardul wove?
3. Why did Jamil want to marry the princess?
4. Why was Jamil lucky to have Sardul?

## Now try these

1. What do you think Sardul's plan might be? Make notes about his plan.
2. Draw a picture of Jamil and Sardul meeting the princess. Add a sentence to show what the princess is thinking.

**Comprehension** Unit 3

# Contemporary tale: 'Tom's Sausage Lion'

**From 'Tom's Sausage Lion' by Michael Morpurgo**

It was Christmas Eve when Tom first saw the lion. His mother had sent him out to fetch the logs, and there was a lion padding through the orchard with a string of sausages hanging from its mouth. Tom ran back inside the house to tell them, but his father just laughed and his mother said he must have been imagining things. He told them and he told them, but they wouldn't even come out to look.

'But it's true,' Tom shouted. 'It was a real lion, I know it was.'

'Perhaps it just looked like a lion,' said his mother. 'After all, it is getting dark outside, isn't it, dear?'

## Get started

Copy the sentences and complete them using words from the story.

1. It was Christmas Eve when _____ first saw the _____ .

2. His mother had sent him _____ to fetch the _____ .

3. There was lion padding through the _____ with a string of _____ hanging from its mouth.

## Try these

Ask a teacher for help with any words in the story you do not know. Write a sentence to answer each question.

1. What day was it?
2. Why had Tom gone out?
3. Why do you think his father and mother wouldn't go and look?
4. Why do you think Tom shouted?

## Now try these

1. Do you think there really was a lion? Why do you think this? Write one or two sentences.
2. Draw a picture of the moment Tom first sees the lion. Add a sentence to show what he is thinking.

# Classic poetry: 'Some One'

Some one came knocking
At my wee, small door;
Some one came knocking,
I'm sure-sure-sure;
I listened, I opened,
I looked to left and right,
But nought there was a-stirring

In the still dark night;
Only the busy beetle
Tap-tapping in the wall,
Only from the forest
The screech-owl's call,
Only the cricket whistling
While the dewdrops fall,
So I know not who came knocking,
At all, at all, at all.

**Walter de la Mare**

## Get started

Copy the lines and complete them using words from the poem.

1. Someone came _____ At my wee, small _____ ;
2. I listened, I opened, I looked to _____ and _____ ,
3. Only the busy _____ Tap-tapping in the _____ ,
4. Only the cricket _____ While the _____ fall,

## Try these

Ask a teacher for help with any words in the poem you do not know. Write a sentence to answer each question.

1. What was tapping in the wall?
2. What was calling in the forest?
3. Why did the speaker of the poem open the door?
4. How do you think the speaker of the poem feels? Why do you think this?

## Now try these

1. Rhyming words are words that sound like each other. The words 'door' and 'sure' are rhyming words in this poem. Find and write the other rhyming words in the poem. Then add other words that sound like them.

2. Draw a picture of the speaker of the poem looking out of the little door. What details from the poem can you include in the picture? Add a sentence to show what the speaker is thinking.

# Comprehension Unit 5

# Classic poetry : 'Who's There?'

Knock, knock!

*Who's there?*
cried the spider.
*Stand and wait!*
But she knew by the
gentle tweak of the web
it was her mate.

Knock, knock!
*Who's there?*
cried the spider.
*Call your name!*
But she knew by the
soft tap-tap on the silk
her spiderlings came.

Knock, knock!
*Who's there?*
cried the spider.
*Who goes by?*
But she knew by the
shaking of her net
it was the fly.

**Judith Nicholls**

## Get started

Copy the lines and complete them using words from the poem.

1. Knock, knock! Who's _____ ? cried the _____ .
2. But she knew by the gentle _____ of the web it was her _____ .
3. But she knew by the _____ of her net it was the _____ .

## Try these

Write a sentence to answer each question about the poem.

1. Who gave a 'soft tap-tap' on the silk?
2. How did the fly move the spider's net?
3. What are the rhyming words in the poem?

## Now try these

1. Note down one idea for a different creature that touches the spider's web. Describe a new way this creature could touch it to let the spider know what it is.
2. Draw and label a picture of the spider on her web with one of her three visitors.

**Comprehension** Unit 6

# Word play: 'Eletelephony'

Once there was an elephant,
Who tried to use the telephant —
No! No! I mean an elephone
Who tried to use the telephone —
(Dear me! I am not certain quite
That even now I've got it right.)

Howe'er it was, he got his trunk
Entangled in the telephunk;
The more he tried to get it free,
The louder buzzed the telephee —
(I fear I'd better drop the song
Of elephop and telephong!)

**Laura E. Richards**

## Get started

Copy the lines and complete them using words from the poem.

1. Once there was an _____ , Who tried to use the _____ —

2. No! No! I mean an elephone Who tried to _____ the _____ —

3. Dear me! I am not certain quite That _____ now I've got it _____ .

## Try these

Ask a teacher for help with any words in the poem you do not know. Write a sentence to answer each question about the poem.

1. What was the elephant really trying to do?
2. What noise did the telephone make?
3. What problem did the elephant really have with his trunk?
4. What are the funny nonsense words in the poem?

## Now try these

1. Explain why the words 'elephant' and 'telephone' can be muddled up.
2. Draw a picture of the elephant trying to use the telephone. Label the picture using all the nonsense words in the poem to show what the poet really meant by these words.

telephant   elephone
telephunk   telephee
elephop   telephong

**Comprehension** Unit 7

# Instructions: Be a snake charmer

Experiment with static electricity in this charming activity.

1. Put a plate on a piece of tissue paper and draw around it. Cut out the circle. Draw a spiral snake inside it, like this.

2. To decorate your snake, use felt-tipped pens to draw a zigzag pattern and eyes. Then cut along the spiral.

3. Rub a plastic ruler fairly hard and fast for half a minute with a scarf or sweater made of wool.

4. Then touch the snake's head with your ruler. Slowly lift the ruler. The snake should uncoil and rise up.

**What's going on?**

When the wool is rubbed against the plastic ruler, it causes particles too small to see to pass from the wool to the ruler. These extra particles on the ruler cause a build-up of static electricity. The static pulls on the tissue paper. The tissue paper is so light that the static on the ruler is strong enough to lift it.

## Get started

Copy the sentences and complete them using words from the instructions.

1. Experiment with static _____ in this _____ activity.

2. Put a plate on a piece of _____ paper and draw _____ it.

3. To decorate your snake, use felt-tipped pens to draw a _____ pattern and _____ .

## Try these

Ask a teacher for help with any words in the instructions you do not know. Write a sentence to answer each question.

1. What is the first thing you have to do?
2. What should you draw with felt-tipped pens?
3. How do the pictures of the snake and ruler help?

## Now try these

1. Make a list of the items you need to do this activity.
2. Draw and label a diagram that could help someone to follow instruction 4.

Review unit 1

# Fiction (story): 'The Stone Cutter'

**From 'The Stone Cutter' by Sean Taylor**

A poor stone cutter
chipped at a rock.
His hammer went TACK
and his chisel went TOCK.

Then a rich man walked past,
in his rich man's clothes.
"I'm just a poor stone cutter,"
the stone cutter said.
"I'd rather be a rich man instead."

And he became a rich man.

Then the emperor rode past with his servants
dressed in blue and gold.
"I'm just a rich man," the stone cutter said.
"I'd rather be the emperor instead."

And he became the emperor.

Then the sun came out.
It was grander and more powerful
than any emperor.

19

## Get started

Copy the sentences and complete them using words from the story.

1. A poor stone cutter _____ at a _____.
2. His hammer went _____ and his chisel went _____.
3. Then a _____ man walked past, in his rich man's _____.
4. "I'd _____ be a rich man _____."

## Try these

Ask a teacher for help with any words in the story you do not know. Write a sentence to answer each question.

1. What was the stone cutter chipping?
2. What tools was the stone cutter using?
3. How do you think the stone cutter became a rich man?
4. Why do you think the stone cutter wanted to be a rich man?

## Now try these

1. What do you think might happen next in the story? Write one or two sentences to share your ideas.
2. Draw a picture of the stone cutter looking at the emperor. Add a sentence to show what the stone cutter is thinking.

## Comprehension Unit 8

# Explanations: 'Seeing the world'

**From 'Your Senses' by Sally Morgan**

We need light to see. Light enters your eye through your pupil, the black spot in the middle of your eye. When the light is dim, your pupil is large, so that lots of light can enter. But when the light is bright, your pupil is small to stop too much light getting in and damaging your eye.

Light passes through your pupil and falls on the back of your eye, where information is sent to your brain. Your brain uses the information to build a picture of what you see.

Light falls on the back of your eye and a message is sent to your brain.

front of eye

light

pupil

The message travels along your optic nerve to your brain.

## Get started

Copy the sentences and complete them using words from the explanation.

1. Light enters your eye through your _____, the black spot in the _____ of your eye.

2. When the light is dim, your pupil is _____, so that lots of _____ can enter.

3. Light passes through your pupil and falls on the _____ of your eye, where information is sent to your _____ .

## Try these

Ask a teacher for help with any words in the explanation you do not know. Write one or two sentences to answer each question.

1. Why do people need light?
2. In this explanation, what is a pupil?
3. Does your eye build up a picture of what you see? If not, what does?
4. How would your pupils change if you went from a dark room into bright sunlight?

## Now try these

1. In your own words, explain what happens to the light when it enters your eye.
2. Draw and label a picture of light entering someone's eye. Use arrows to show the light. Use the explanation text to find the details.

**Comprehension** Unit 9

# Non-chronological report: Gerbils

### What is a gerbil?

Gerbils are small, mouse-like animals with hairy tails and strong back legs. They are clean and fun-loving, and make excellent pets.

### Appearance

Gerbils are about 10 cm (4 in.) tall – larger than a mouse, but smaller than a rat.

### Desert diggers

Wild gerbils and their relatives come from desert regions. They live in groups called colonies, inside huge networks of tunnels that they dig in the sand.

### Need to gnaw

Like rats and hamsters, gerbils are rodents. These are animals with two pairs of strong front teeth for gnawing. The name 'gerbil' comes from the Arabic word 'jarbou', meaning 'rodent'.

## Get started

Copy the sentences and complete them using words from the report.

1. Gerbils are small, mouse-like animals with _____ tails and _____ back legs.
2. Gerbils are about 10 cm (4 in.) tall – larger than a _____ , but a smaller than a _____ .

## Try these

Ask a teacher for help with any words in the report you do not know. Write one or two sentences to answer each question.

1. How could you tell the difference between a gerbil and a mouse?
2. In which parts of the world do wild gerbils live?
3. Why does the writer think that a gerbil would make a good pet?
4. What are the sub-headings in this report? Why are they used?

## Now try these

1. If you wanted to get a gerbil as a pet, what other information might you like to know? Write at least three questions that you could ask.
2. Draw and label a picture of a gerbil. Use the report to find the details. Write three other facts from the report about the gerbil.

# Fairy tale: 'Rumpelstiltskin'

**From 'Rumpelstiltskin' by Abie Longstaff**

Daisy sat and wept. She did not know how to spin straw into gold! She was so embarrassed.
The king would never marry her now!
"Everyone will laugh at me again," she sobbed.
"Oh help!"
Suddenly a trap door opened in the floor and out jumped a goblin.

"I will help you," he promised, "if you give me your necklace."
Daisy agreed and, to her amazement, the goblin spun the straw into gold.
In the morning, the king was happy.
But seeing the gold made him greedy.
He took Daisy to a bigger room filled with straw.
"I want more gold by morning," he demanded.
Again Daisy called for help.

## Get started

Copy the sentences and complete them using words from the story.

1. She did not know how to _____ straw into _____!
2. Suddenly, a trap door _____ in the floor and out jumped a _____.
3. In the _____, the king was _____.
4. He took Daisy to a _____ room filled with _____.

## Try these

Ask a teacher for help with any words in the story you do not know. Write one or two sentences to answer each question.

1. What did the goblin do to help Daisy?
2. What did Daisy give the goblin in return?
3. Why does Daisy think the king will never marry her?
4. What kind of person do you think the king was?

## Now try these

1. What do you think will happen next in this story? Write one or two sentences to explain your ideas.
2. Draw a picture of Daisy watching the goblin spinning the straw into gold. Add a sentence to show what Daisy is thinking.

# Traditional tale: 'The Great Chapatti Chase'

**From 'The Great Chapatti Chase' by Penny Dolan**

The woman rolled the dough flat and turned it, again and again, until she had made a perfectly round chapatti.

The woman smiled. "My, what a handsome little chapatti," she said. "You'll be delicious to eat!" And – flip, flap! – she flung that chapatti on to the hot iron stove.

However – believe it or not! – as soon as this little chapatti felt the fire, he puffed out his fat round cheeks and grinned.

"Delicious to eat?" he replied, laughing. "No, no, you silly woman! I'm not staying to be eaten!"

With that, he jumped off the stove and rolled right out of the door, singing for all to hear:

"Run, run as fast as you can! You can't catch me, I'm Chapatti Man!"

## Get started

Copy the sentences and complete them using words from the story.

1. The woman rolled the _____ flat and turned it, again and again, until she had made a perfectly _____ chapatti.
2. "My, what a _____ little _____," she said.
3. However – believe it or not! – as soon as this little chapatti felt the _____, he puffed out his fat round _____ and grinned.
4. "No, no, you silly woman! I'm not _____ to be _____!"

## Try these

Ask a teacher for help with any words in the story you do not know. Write one or two sentences to answer each question.

1. Why did the woman turn the dough 'again and again'?
2. What did the woman think about the chapatti?
3. Why did the woman put the chapatti on the hot iron stove?
4. Why did the chapatti run away?

## Now try these

1. What do you think will happen next in this story? Write one or two sentences to explain your ideas.
2. Draw a picture of the chapatti jumping off the hot iron stove. Add a sentence to show what he is thinking.

**Comprehension** Unit 12

# Contemporary tale: 'Mountain Mona'

**From 'Mountain Mona' by Vivian French**

Mona frowned. "Are you a lion?"
"YES," said the lion. "What did you think I was?"
"Well," said Mona, "I thought you were a sunflower."
"A SUNFLOWER?" The lion looked angry.
"I'm a BIG FIERCE LION!"
Mona looked at the lion more closely.
"I thought you were a BIG sunflower," she said.

The lion sat down. "This is terrible," he said.
"How can I scare anyone if I look like a sunflower?"
Mona thought hard.
"Maybe I'm no good at being scared," she said, quietly.
"After all, I'm no good at jumping or leaping or climbing or scrambling. Maybe I'm no good at being scared either."

29

## Get started

Copy the sentences and complete them using words from the story.

1. "Well," said Mona, "I _____ you were a _____."

2. Mona looked at the _____ more _____.

3. The lion sat _____. "This is _____," he said.

4. "Maybe I'm no _____ at being _____," she said, quietly.

## Try these

Ask a teacher for help with any words in the story you do not know. Write one or two sentences to answer each question.

1. What did Mona think the lion was?

2. How did the lion feel about this?

3. Why do you think the lion wanted to scare people?

4. What was Mona thinking about when she thought hard?

## Now try these

1. How do you think Mona and the lion could help one another? Write one or two sentences to explain your ideas.

2. Draw a picture of things you are good at doing. Add one or two sentences to explain your picture.

**Comprehension** Unit 13

# Classic poetry: 'If'

**From 'If' by Mij Kelly**

If you can keep your head when alligators
are stealing bedclothes from your bed
and keep your cool when, 15 minutes later,
a greedy hippo eats your eggy bread …

If you can walk to school with your big brother
although he really is a dreadful sight,
and wave goodbye, although your lovely mother
has turned into a monster overnight …

If you can cross the playground in the morning –
a playground full of fearsome dinosaurs –
and keep on walking when, without a warning,
they raise their heads and roar and roar and roar …

## Get started

Copy the lines and complete them using words from the poem.

1. If you can keep your head when _____ are stealing _____ from your bed
2. and keep your _____ when, 15 minutes later, a greedy _____ eats your eggy bread
3. If you can _____ to school with your big _____
4. and wave _____ although your _____ mother has turned into a monster overnight

## Try these

Ask a teacher for help with any words in the poem you do not know. Write one or two sentences to answer each question about the poem.

1. Where does the poem suggest there may be dinosaurs?

2. What does the poem suggest the dinosaurs may do?

3. How do you think the speaker of the poem would feel when crossing the playground?

4. Do you think all the things described in this poem are real? Why or why not?

## Now try these

1. This is only a part of a longer poem. What else do you think might happen later in the poem? Write one or two sentences to share your ideas.

2. Draw a picture of something described in the poem. Add one or two sentences to explain how you think the speaker feels about it.

**Comprehension** Unit 14

# Contemporary poetry: 'Market Day'

**From 'Catching Flies' by June Crebbin**

On Saturdays I'm up at four
To go with Bill who lives next door,
To market.
And while I'm doing what I can
Unloading crates, he takes the van
To park it.

There's heaps of grapefruits big as suns,
And oranges and purple plums
And berries —
Raspberries, strawberries, damsons — lots
Of peaches, pears, ripe apricots
And cherries.

I love arranging nectarines
And polishing their shiny skins
For selling.
But best of all I like the sound
When market traders all around
Start yelling!

Then we're busy all day long
And Bill says I'm his Number One
Best Mate,
And even when we pack away
I'm thinking of next market day —
Can't wait!

33

## Get started

Copy the lines and complete them using words from the poem.

1. On Saturdays I'm up at ──────

   To go with ────── who lives next door

2. There's heaps of ────── big as suns

   And oranges and ────── plums

3. But best of all I ────── the sound

   When market ────── all around

   Start yelling!

4. Then we're busy ────── day long

   And Bill says I'm his ────── One

## Try these

Ask a teacher for help with any words in the poem you do not know. Write one or two sentences to answer each question about the poem.

1. How many different kinds of fruit can you count in the poem?

2. What does the speaker do at the market to help Bill?

3. Why do you think Bill takes the speaker to the market with him?

4. Why do you think the speaker enjoys going to the market?

## Now try these

1. Rhyming words are words that sound like each other. The words 'four' and 'door' are rhyming words in this poem. Find and write the other rhyming words.

2. Draw a picture of the market. What details from the poem can you include in the picture? Add a sentence to show what the speaker is thinking.

Review unit 2

# Non-fiction (information text): 'Landmarks of the World'

**From 'Landmarks of the World' by Helen Chapman**

**What is a landmark?**

A landmark is a well-known object or feature of a place that is easy to see and recognise.

It helps people to understand where they are in the world.

Within each of Earth's seven continents are man-made landmarks. Let's visit some of them!

**Africa: The Great Sphinx and the Great Pyramid, Giza, Egypt**

This pyramid is a tomb for a dead ruler called a pharaoh.

It is the largest pyramid ever built.

This statue, with a lion's body and a man's head, guards the tomb.

**Antarctica: Halley 6 Research Station**

Although Antarctica is almost completely covered by ice, scientists work here all year round.

## Get started

Copy the sentences and complete them using words from the text.

1. A landmark is a well-known _____ or feature of a place that is _____ to see and recognise.
2. It helps _____ to understand where they are in the _____.
3. Within each of Earth's _____ continents are _____ landmarks.
4. This _____ is a tomb for a dead ruler called a _____.

## Try these

Ask a teacher for help with any words in the text you do not know. Write a sentence to answer each question.

1. What is a landmark?
2. What type of body does the sphinx guarding the pyramid have?
3. For how much of the year do the scientists work at the Halley 6 Research Station?
4. Why do you think people like to visit landmarks?

## Now try these

1. What do you think is meant by 'man-made' landmarks? Write one or two sentences to explain.
2. Draw and label a picture of the Great Pyramid and the Great Sphinx that guards it.

# Recount: 'A Letter to New Zealand'

**From 'A Letter to New Zealand' by Alison Hawes**

Jack lives in the UK. He is writing a letter to his penpal, Tama, in New Zealand. Jack writes Tama's name and address on the envelope. His letter is going on a long journey. New Zealand is on the other side of the world from the UK.

**Posting the letter**

Jack buys a stamp at the post office. The cost of the stamp pays for the letter to go to New Zealand by airmail. Post for New Zealand can be sent by sea too, but airmail is quicker. Jack puts the stamp on his letter. Then Jack pops his letter in the postbox. It will take about five days to reach Tama.

**Collecting the letter**

Later, a postman collects all the post from the postbox. He takes all the post to a big sorting office.

**Sorting the letters**

At the sorting office, the letters go into a big machine. First it sorts the letters by size. Next it puts the letters the right way up and stamps them with a postmark.

## Get started

Copy the sentences and complete them using words from the text.

1. Jack writes Tama's _____ and _____ on the envelope.
2. The cost of the stamp pays for the _____ to go to New Zealand by _____.
3. Then Jack _____ his letter in the _____.
4. At the _____ office, the letters go into a big _____.

## Try these

Ask a teacher for help with any words in the text you do not know. Write one or two sentences to answer each question.

1. To which country is Jack sending his letter?
2. Why does Jack need to buy a stamp?
3. What does the machine do to the letters?
4. Why do you think letters need to be sorted?

## Now try these

1. Think about what happens to the letter after it has been sorted at the sorting office. Write three questions you could ask about what happens next.
2. Draw and label a diagram to show all or part of the journey of a letter, using information from the text.

# Instructions: 'How to Make Storybooks'

**From 'How to Make Storybooks' by Ros Asquith**

**Planning**

When you have your idea, you can start to plan your story.

1. Make a list of the characters who will be in your book. The characters could be animals, pirates, aliens – or they could be you and your friends. It's your choice.

2. Make a list of the things that will happen to them.

3. Think of a really good way to start your story.

4. Then think of a really good ending.

5. Then work out the bits in between. You can change your beginning and your ending later, if you want to.

6. Make up a good title for the book so that other people will want to read it.

## Get started

Copy the sentences and complete them using words from the instructions.

1. When you have your _____, you can start to plan your _____.
2. The characters could be animals, _____, aliens – or they could be you and your _____.
3. Think of a _____ good way to _____ your story.
4. Make up a good _____ for the book so that other people will want to_____ it.

## Try these

Ask a teacher for help with any words in the instructions you do not know. Write one or two sentences to answer each question.

1. What is the first instruction?
2. Should you think of the beginning, middle or end of the story first?
3. Can you change parts of your story later?
4. Why does the book need a good title?

## Now try these

1. What do you think would be the hardest part of making your own storybook? Write one or two sentences to share your ideas.
2. Draw a comic strip of someone following these instructions. Use one panel for each instruction.

# Explanation: 'How does a magnetic drawing board work?'

**From 'How Does it Work?' by Sylvia Karavis and Gill Matthews**

You write on a magnetic drawing board with a magnetic pen. You move the sliding magnet up and down to rub out what you have written.

*magnetic pen*

*sliding magnet*

## Inside a magnetic drawing board

The screen has three parts. The front and back parts are pieces of plastic. The middle part is also plastic and looks like a honeycomb. It is filled with a thick liquid. In the liquid are tiny magnetic pieces.

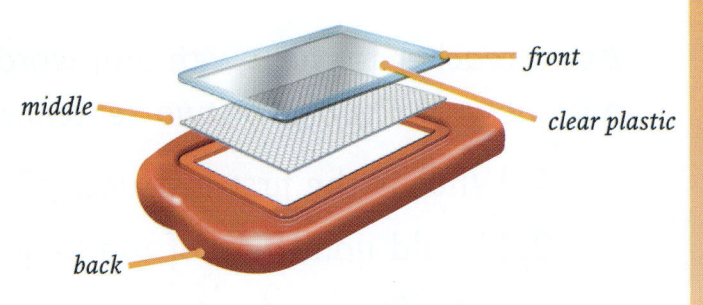

*middle*

*front*

*clear plastic*

*back*

When you draw on the front screen with the magnetic pen, the pieces are attracted to the top of the liquid. This means that you can see them through the screen.

## Get started

Copy the sentences and complete them using words from the explanation.

1. You write on a magnetic _____ board with a _____ pen.
2. The front and _____ parts are pieces of _____.
3. In the liquid are _____ magnetic _____.
4. When you draw on the front _____ with the magnetic pen, the pieces are _____ to the top of the liquid.

## Try these

Ask a teacher for help with any words in the explanation you do not know. Write one or two sentences to answer each question.

1. How many parts does the screen have?
2. What is in the liquid?
3. What happens when you draw on the front screen?
4. What parts make up the magnetic drawing board?

## Now try these

1. What else would you like to know about how a magnetic drawing board works? Write three questions.
2. In your own words, explain how magnets help the drawing board to work.

# Non-chronological report: 'The Cloud Forest'

**From 'The Cloud Forest' by Nic Bishop**

**What is a cloud forest?**

A cloud forest is a very special type of forest. It grows high in the mountains where the trees are nearly always covered in clouds. Clouds blow through the trees, wetting their leaves and branches, and rain falls almost every day.

These forests are rare because they only grow on the cloudiest mountain ranges. You can see them in different places around the world, in tropical parts of Asia, Africa, Australia and the Americas.

Cloud forests are rich in plants and animals that live nowhere else on Earth.

They also have secrets to tell us.

## Get started

Copy the sentences and complete them using words from the report.

1. A cloud _____ is a very special _____ of forest.

2. It grows high in the _____ where the trees are nearly always _____ in clouds.

3. These forests are _____ because they only grow on the _____ mountain ranges.

4. They also _____ secrets to _____ us.

## Try these

Ask a teacher for help with any words in the report you do not know. Write one or two sentences to answer each question.

1. In which parts of the world can you see cloud forests?

2. Why are cloud forests rare?

3. Why do cloud forests grow high up in the mountains?

4. What do you think the last sentence means?

## Now try these

1. What else would you like to know about cloud forests? Write three questions.

2. Use the text to imagine how a cloud forest might look. Draw a picture of it and add labels.

**Comprehension** Unit 19

# Contemporary tale: 'Tiger's Tale'

**From 'Tiger's Tale' by Michaela Morgan**

Tiger was not a very special cat. He had no particular talents and he lived nowhere in particular, but he could settle down anywhere …
anywhere at all.

He perched in tall trees beneath the stars.
He snoozed on the hot tops of cars.

He lounged in sunny spaces in the park and prowled on rooftops in the dark.

Yes, Tiger could settle anywhere.

But he did have his favourite places.
One of them was the library.

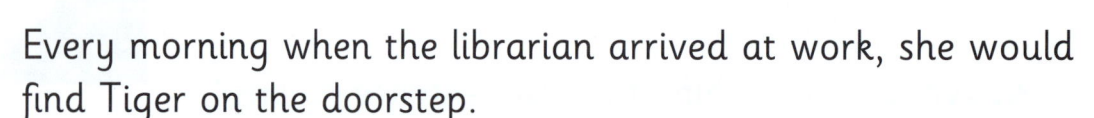

Every morning when the librarian arrived at work, she would find Tiger on the doorstep.

She'd unlock the library door and he would pad in and make himself at home.

## Get started

Copy the sentences and complete them using words from the story.

1. Tiger was _____ a very _____ cat.
2. He _____ in tall trees beneath the _____.
3. He snoozed on the _____ tops of _____.
4. Every morning when the _____ arrived at work, she would find Tiger on the _____.

## Try these

Ask a teacher for help with any words in the story you do not know. Write one or two sentences to answer each question.

1. What type of animal is Tiger?
2. Where did Tiger lounge?
3. What does it mean that Tiger could 'settle anywhere'?
4. How do you think the librarian felt about Tiger?

## Now try these

1. What trouble could Tiger make at the library? Write one or two sentences to share your ideas.
2. Draw and label a picture of Tiger settled in one of the places described. Add one or two sentences to describe where he is.

# Traditional tale: 'The Brave Baby'

**From 'The Brave Baby' by Malachy Doyle**

The Indian chief was brave and fierce, so many people were afraid of him.

But a wise old woman said,
"I know someone who is not afraid of you."

The Indian chief was surprised.
"Who is this man?" he cried. "Show him to me!"

The old woman took him to her tent.

"Where is this man?" said the chief.
"I cannot see him."

"It is not a man," said the old woman.
"It is Wasso, the baby girl."
Wasso sat on a blanket, playing with a stick.

"Why is this baby not afraid of me?" said the chief.
"Everyone is afraid of me!"

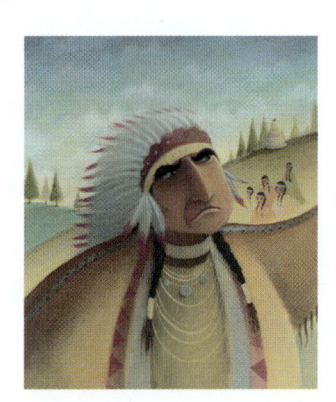

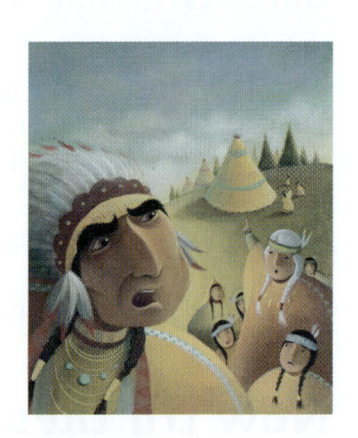

## Get started

Copy the sentences and complete them using words from the story.

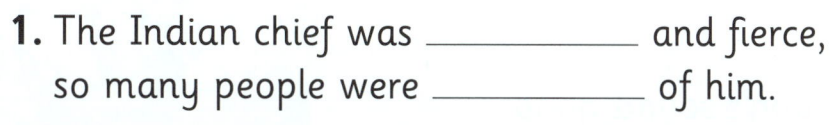

1. The Indian chief was _____ and fierce, so many people were _____ of him.
2. But a _____ old woman said, "I know _____ who is not afraid of you."
3. The old _____ took him to her _____.
4. Wasso sat on a _____, playing with a _____.

## Try these

Ask a teacher for help with any words in the story you do not know. Write one or two sentences to answer each question.

1. Why were people afraid of the Indian chief?
2. How did the Indian chief feel when the old woman said she knew someone who was not afraid?
3. Why do you think the old woman told him this?
4. Why do you think Wasso was not afraid of the chief?

## Now try these

1. What do you think might happen next in the story? Write one or two sentences to share your ideas.
2. Draw a picture of the Indian chief meeting Wasso. Add one or two sentences to show what the chief is thinking.

**Review unit 3**

# Poetry: 'Bugs'

**From 'Bugs' by Sam McBratney**

Bugs!
I agree, we don't sound good.
We cause more trouble than we should.

But ... let me tell you this about us,
People on Earth can't do without us.
In fact, you owe us such a lot!
If we weren't here to make things rot ...

... the piles of stuff you throw away
Would just get bigger every day.
Yes! We make things rot!
We make them *smell!*

Apple cores, potato skins,
All the scraps in all your bins –
We get to work and cause decay.
In time we rot it all away.

Rubbish mountains there would be,
If you didn't have my friends and me.

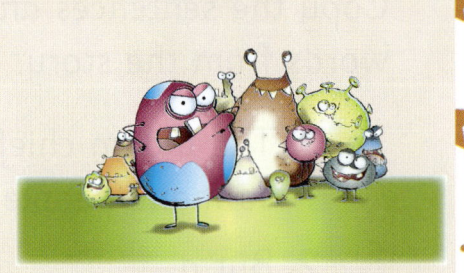

## Get started

Copy the sentences and complete them using words from the poem.

1. We cause _____ trouble than we _____.
2. People on _____ can't do _____ us.
3. In fact, _____ owe _____ such a lot!
4. We get to _____ and cause _____.

## Try these

Ask a teacher for help with any words in the poem you do not know. Write a sentence to answer each question.

1. Who can't do without bugs?
2. What do the bugs do to things we throw away?
3. What examples of food scraps are given in the poem?
4. Why would there be rubbish mountains if there weren't any bugs?

## Now try these

1. How do you feel about bugs? Write one or two sentences to share your ideas.
2. Draw and label a picture of the bugs eating food scraps. Add a sentence to show what the bugs do.